GEO

Pebble Plus

Life around the World
Families in Many Cultures

by Heather Adamson

Consulting Editor: Gail Saunders-Smith, PhD

Capstone press

Mankato, Minnesota

Pebble Plus is published by Capstone Press,
151 Good Counsel Drive, P.O. Box 669, Mankato, Minnesota 56002.
www.capstonepress.com

1 2 3 4 5 6 12 11 10 09 08 07

Library of Congress Cataloging-in-Publication Data
Adamson, Heather, 1974–
    Families in many cultures / by Heather Adamson.
    p. cm.— (Pebble plus. Life around the world)
    Summary: "Simple text and photographs present families from many cultures"—Provided by publisher.
    Includes bibliographical references and index.
    ISBN-13: 978-1-4296-0019-4 (hardcover)
    ISBN-10: 1-4296-0019-5 (hardcover)
    1. Family—Cross-cultural studies—Juvenile literature. I. Title. II. Series.
HQ744.A33 2008
306.85—dc22   2006101951

Editorial Credits
Sarah L. Schuette, editor; Alison Thiele, set designer; Kara Birr, photo researcher

Photo Credits
© WOLFGANG KAEHLER 2007/www.wkaehlerphoto.com, 19
Corbis/Annie Griffiths Belt, 9; Simon Marcus, 17
iStockphoto/Chris Johnson, cover; Cliff Parnell, 21
Peter Arnold/Mark Edwards, 15; Russell Gordon, 11; Sean Sprague, 5
Shutterstock/Jason Stitt, 1
SuperStock Inc./Anton Vengo, 7; Steve Vidler, 13

Note to Parents and Teachers

The Life around the World set supports national social studies standards related to
culture and geography. This book describes and illustrates families in many cultures. The
images support early readers in understanding the text. The repetition of words and
phrases helps early readers learn new words. This book also introduces early readers
to subject-specific vocabulary words, which are defined in the Glossary section. Early
readers may need assistance to read some words and to use the Table of Contents,
Glossary, Read More, Internet Sites, and Index sections of the book.

Table of Contents

Living Together

Families of all sizes
live around the world.
How is your family
like other families?

Guatemala

Children around the world
live with their parents.
Sometimes grandparents
live with them too.

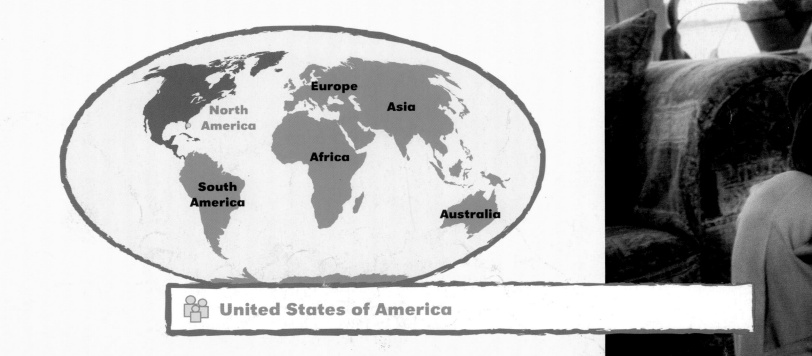

North
America

Europe

Asia

Africa

South
America

Australia

United States of America

Aunts, uncles, and cousins
are parts of families too.
They may live far away.

North America

Europe

Asia

Africa

South America

Australia

Israel

8

Around the House

Families help each other.

A mother in China

helps her son

with homework.

North America

Europe

Asia

Africa

South America

Australia

China

Families share meals.

A family in New Zealand

cooks and eats together.

Family Fun

Families celebrate holidays.
A family in Africa dances
and visits with relatives.

North America
Europe
Asia
Africa
South America
Australia

Mauritania

Families celebrate birthdays.
A father in China blows out
his birthday candles.

North
America

Europe

Asia

Africa

South
America

Australia

China

Families play together.

A family in Germany surfs

on their vacation.

Europe

North
America

Asia

Africa

South
America

Australia

Germany

Your Family

Families hug
and laugh together.
How does your family
have fun?

20

Glossary

celebrate—to do something fun on a special occasion; families often gather together to celebrate birthdays, holidays, or other important events.

holiday—a festival, religious celebration, or day of memory

meal—the food that is served and eaten at certain times of the day such as breakfast or lunch

relative—a member of your family; your parents, grandparents, aunts, uncles, and cousins are relatives.

surf—to ride on waves using a surfboard

vacation—a time of rest from school, work, or a trip away from home

Read More

Easterling, Lisa. *Families.* Our Global Community. Chicago: Heinemann, 2007.

Kuklin, Susan. *Families.* New York: Hyperion Books, 2006.

Robertson, J. Jean. *Meet My Grandparents.* Vero Beach, Fla.: Rourke, 2007.

Internet Sites

FactHound offers a safe, fun way to find Internet sites related to this book. All of the sites on FactHound have been researched by our staff.

Here's how:

1. Visit *www.facthound.com*

2. Choose your grade level.

3. Type in this book ID **1429600195**
   for age-appropriate sites. You may also browse subjects by clicking on letters, or by clicking on pictures and words.

4. Click on the **Fetch It** button.

FactHound will fetch the best sites for you!

Index

Word Count: 114
Grade: 1
Early-Intervention Level: 12